TOC \h \u \z \n

Thepoweroflove:

Truelovegivesandserves.

By

JessicaStevensons

Tableofcontent

Introduction

Toloveatallistobevulnerable.Loveanythingandyourheartwillundoubtedlybewrungandpossiblybebroken.Ifyouwanttomakesureofkeepingyourheartintact,youmustsurrenderyourhearttonoone,noteventoananimal.TheWrapIgentlyroundwithhobbiesandminordelights.Avoidallentanglements;lockitupsafeinthecasketorcoffinofyourselfishness.Butinthatcasket-safe,dark,unmoving,airlessitwilltransform.Itwillnotbebroken;itwillbecomeunbreakable,impenetrable,irredeemable.

Recently,Ihavegrownsoinlovewithmyspiritualpathandgrowththat Ihavenotfelttheneedforaspouse.Perhapsitisagoodthingas Iwouldneverwanttoloveoutof“need”anyway.Ihavebecomesoholytomyselfthattheresimplyhasnotbeenaplaceordesireforanyoneelse.Ilovethemannerthat Ilove:fearlessly.Iintendtokeeplovingthatway.Itwasforthisreasonthat Iresolvedtogoitalone:noromance,nodating,nopretenddating,noalmostdating,no“sugar-free”confectionery.Justasacredtimewithmyself.Ihaveinvestednotimeinthis.Thiscouldallchangebetweenthetime Ipostthi spieceanditsfirstreader.Itrust myselftoknow.Whatisinarguablyevident,isthenexttime,ifthereisone,willbenothingshortofsacrosanct.

Chapter1

TheInfluenceOfLove

BrothersEthanandNathanhavestrikingphysicalsimilaritiesbutleadquitedifferentlifestyles. EventhoughtheirdevotedChristianparentshadbroughtthemupinthefearandinstructionoftheLord.Whenthetwinswereroughlyyoungadults,theirfatherandhisyoungerchildrendiedin anautoaccident,leavingthetwinsandtheirmotheralone.Ethanhaddecidedtoleadawaywardlife(streetfighting,stealing,hooliganism,drinking,andallsorts).

Soonaftertheirfatherpassedaway,Ethancompletelylostcontrol.Itappearedasthoughanyremainingself-controlhehadduetohisfather'sdreadhadabruptlyevaporated.Heimmediatelystartedlivinghislifeaccordingtohispreferences.Ethanhaddisplayedmoresignsofrestlessnessthanhisbrother Nathaneversincetheyweretoddlers.Anddespitetheirbest efforts,theirparentswereunabletochangehisbehavior.Hehadspentmultipletimesinandoutofprisonbeforeturningeighteen.Nothingtheydidhadanyeffectonhim.Evenhistwinbrother'ssincereappealsforhimtoacceptJesusintohisheartfailedtoswayhim.Infact,ratherthantransforminghim,itjustintensifiedhisanimosityforNathanandcausedhimtobecomemoreandmoreentrenchedinhismisdeeds.

Oneday,whileintoxicated,Ethanviolentlyshovedhismothertothefloorassheattemptedtocounselhimaboutstartingover.Shespentseveralweeksinthehospital.Althoughitwouldhavebe enexpectedthathismother'sprotractedbattleforsurvivalwouldhavesoftenedEthan,hebecamemorerecklessinhisbehavior.Buteventhoughshewasill,theirmother,Sarah,neverstoppedworryingaboutEthan'swell-being.ShewantedhersontobecomeaChristiandespitehersuffering.Howprofoundthelove!

Nathan,likehistwinbrother,neverstoppedprayingforhim.HeneverlostfaiththatEthanwouldgrowtolovetheLordasmuchasheandtheirmotherdid.Asaresult,helovedhimmoreandprayedforhimmorefervently despiteEthan'songoingdisplaysofhatredandbrutalityagainsthim.N ow,itsohappenedthatEthanattendedabirthdaypartyonacertainnight.Hesoonfeltboredbecausehispartnerwaspreoccupiedwithtakingcareofthevisitorsshortlyafterhehadeatenthere.Sohewentlookingforanotherwomantohangoutwith.Thewoman'sboyfriendbecameenragedbythisandbegantoarguewithhim.Ethanstabbedhisattackertodeathafterbreakingabottleinaninstant.Ethandidn'trealizewhathehadjustdoneuntilhefeltbloodonhisshirt.However,bythispoint,people'sattentionwasfocusedonthem.Hehurriedlypushedtheyoungmanawayfromhimandsprintedforthedoor.

Manyindividualssoonfollowedinhiswake.Henearlygothitbyapolicevanonpatrolthatnightasheenteredthestreets.Hewasdrenchedinblood,andtheysoonobservedotherindividualspursuinghim.Theyjoinedthepursuitaswell.

WhileEthanwasbeingdraggedtohellandyellingforaid,Nathan,whowassleeping,hadanightmareaboutthesituation.Hesuddenlyawoketothesoundofsomeoneknockingonthedoor.Ashehurriedlyapproachedthedoor,hewasshockedtodiscoverEthandrenchedinbloodwithascaredexpressiononhisface.Ethandescribedwhathadoccurredatt hepartyandhowhewasbeingpursuedbythecopsandseveralpartygoerswhilegaspingforair.Afterhefinishedhisstory,Nathanrequestedhimtoremovehisblood-stainedclothingandofferedhimhiscleanshirttowearwhilehedidso.Theyhadjustfinisheddressingwhenagroupofmeninuniformbargedthroughthedoor.WithinminutesEthanwaswatchingfromthewindowasNathanwastakenawayinaheavilyguardedpolicevan.

Nathanwasgivenacourtdate.Hedeclinedtochallengetheprosecutor'sassertionincourt.Hedeclinedtorepresenthimself,hir eanattorneytoargueonhisbehalf,ortaketheonethegovernmentoffered.Thejudgewasenragedbyhissilence,andhegavehimahangingdeathsentence.Whenhismotherattemptedtolearnwhathadhappened—knowingfullwellthatNathanwasincapableofcommittingsuchacrime—hewouldonlyrespondbysayingthatitwasaprivatematterbetweenhimself,Ethan,andGod.Ironically,Ethanneveroncemadeittohisbrother'scourtappearance.Hewashavingtoomuchfuntoworryaboutwhatmighthappentohisbrother.

Butonthedayofhisexecution, Nathanaskedforapenandpaper,andhescribbledthenotestohisbrotherbelow.

DearEthan,
Iamsendingyouthisletterfromthelocationofmyimpendingexecutionbecausethejudgehasalreadygivenmethedeathpenalty.Bythetimeyoureceivethisletter,Iwouldhavepassedaway. Doyoustillrecalltheeveningyoustabbedayoungmantodeathandfledhomewithbloodonyourshirt?FearovercamemeasIstoodandlistenedtoyoudescribewhathappenedatthepartythatnight.Ihadbeendeeplyconsideri

ngwhatwouldhappentoyouifyoudiedwithoutChrist.Iwasmotivatedbylovetotakeyourbloodyclothingandwearit.Ididn'tgiveadamnabouttheconsequencesofmyactions.Imerelywantedyoutohaveachancetoturnfromyoursinandfindsalvation.BeyondanythingIhavedoneforyou,Ethan,rememberthesufferingandmiseryJesusenduredforyourbenefit.Hesacrificedhislifesothatyoucouldgetthecrownoflife.Jesushasgivenyousomuch.WhatwillyoudotopleaseHim?Don'tletthissacrificegotowaste.Donotletmydeathcausemymother'ssorrowtobeinvain.

Ibegyou,myreader,withaheav
yheartandabrokenspirit,togiv
eyourlifetoJesus.Thisreprese
ntsalifebeinggivenupforanoth
er.I'mexcitedtoseeyouinheav
en.

YoursTruly,
Nathan

Ethansobbedbitterlyashefinis
hedreadingthenote.Theletterh
elpedhimgrasptheextentofhis
brother'sloveforHimaswellast
hesignificanceofChrist'ssacri
ficialdeathforHiscause.Hetho
ughtbackonallthecruelthings
hehaddonetohisbrotherandall
thetimeshehadrejectedGod'sr

equestsforhishearttobegivenovertoHim.HewasdeeplyconcernedtolearnthatNathandidnothingbutlovehisbrotherandstriveforhisultimatewelfaredespitehisbrutaltreatmentofhim.WhilesincerelypleadingwithGodforforgivenessandpromisingtoserveHimfortherestofhislife,hebrokedownintears.

Chapter2

SupremacyOfLove

Althoughloveispreferabletofaithandhope,botharewonderfultraitsandabilities.How?Inthistext,Paulcontrastslovewithspiritualgiftsandaddressthepropensityofpeopletomaketheirsuccessesandgiftsthecenterofattention.Foratleastsixreasons,loveisvastlysuperiortofaithandhope.

1.LovefocusesonGodHimself,whereasfaithconcentratesonGod'srevelation.Arelationshipofadmirationandreverenceis sparkedbylove.Ofcourse,faithcanelicitthesamedevotionandworship,butfaithisalsocapableofexistingindependentlyoftheseemotions.

2.LoveispreferablebecauseitplacesmoreemphasisonGodHimselfthanhope,whichcentersonspendingeternitywithGodinaflawlessenvironment.Onecanhopeforsomeoneeveniftheydon'tlovethem,butsomeonetheylovealwayshashopeforthem.

3.God'snature,notthatofman,iswheretrueagapelovecomesfrom.GottistLiebe.

4.Godgivesustrueloveasagift.Onlyasamanlearnstounderstan

ndGod'slovecanheexperience truelove.

5.Experienceandnatureitselfd emonstratethatalthoughloveg rowspeoplemorethananyothe rtraitorgift,faithandhopedoas well.

6.ApersonmayhavefaithinGo dbutstillfeelsuperiortoothers. Hisreligioncouldmakehimco nceitedandhaughty.Truelove, however,hasnoflaws.Loveisu nfailingandneverfallsshort.L oveentailskindness,sacrifice, andselflessness.

Oh,thestrengthofreallove!Th emostuneducatedbarbarians mayunderstandandrespondtot hisuniversallanguageonanins tinctuallevel.Thatmagicalgoldenkeyfitsalllocksperfectly.Thatpotenttreatmenthassoftenedmanyacoldheart,tamedmanyaferociousbeast,anddestroyedmanyinsurmountableobstacles!

Lovetrulyappealstousinawaythatnothingelsedoes.Itsucceedswhereallotherattemptshavefailed.Manypeoplewhobyusinglogicappearedtobebeyondsavinghavebeenwonoverbyreceivingtendercare.Manypeoplewhowereonceobstinate,apathetic,anddistantagainstthemessageofredemptionhavebeensoftenedbythegentletouchofcompassion.TheBiblestatesthat

"Deepcallethuntodeep"(Psalm42.7).Thepotentialforsensitivitylonghiddenorseeminglynonexistentintherecessesoftherecipient'sheartmustfinallybecalledoutbythelovesogreatastosacrificially,consistently,andpersistentlycarefortheneedsofanother.EventhoughtherearemanyforcesatplayonEarth,loveisthemostpowerfulofthemall.Everythingispracticallyfeasiblewhenthereislove.Victoryoverlife'schallengescanbeattained(SeethecaseofJobinJob42:10).Familytragediescanbeavoided(Abigail,1Samuel25).Life-
changingbreakthroughscanbe

attained(David,1Samuel30:1-19).Nationaldisasterscanbeavoided(Esther,Esther4-9).Posteritycanbepreserved(Ruth,Ruth1:16-17;4:13-22).Historycanbemade(MaryofBethany,Mark14:3-9).

Everyoneinourdayrecognizesthepowerandeffectivenessoflove,whichiswhyeveryonelongstobeloved,acceptedandtreatedwithregard.Butdespitehowstrangeitmaysound,inasocietywherebitterrivalries,festeringwounds,andscorchingselfishnessabound,thepathofloveisfrequentlytheoneleasttaken.Themajoritypreferstofollowthepathofselfishness,wickedness, hatred,coldness,andacrimony overthewonderfulrouteoflove inthemajorityofsituations,incl udingthoseinvolvingrelations hipsbetweenindividuals,famil ies,workplaces,andevenpeopl ewhosharethesamereligiousb eliefs.

Theexplanationseemsplausib le.SincetheFall,man'snatureh asevolvedintoonethatisviciou sandself-
centered.ThedesireforSatanto replaceGodwasmotivatedbys elf-
interest.Andafterthefirstcoupl e'sdisobedience,hetransmitte dthesamenaturetoman.Becau seofthis,noneofthemoptedtot

akeresponsibilityforthedisob
edience;instead,theypreferred
toassignblametoprotecttheiri
nterests.Andtothisday,thisist
hemainreasonwhythereareso
manycrisesinfamilies,commu
nities,andcountries.Ourworld
wouldbeamuchmorepeaceful
andenjoyableplacetoliveifonl
ypeoplewouldacceptandsprea
dtheloveofGod

Chapter3

SanctityOfLove

Bytheway,it'scrucialtoexplai
nwhattrueloveisbecausedespi
tehowprevalentcruelty,indiff

erence,andselfishnessare,pra cticallyeveryonebelievesthey possessthisvirtue,thequeenof virtues.However,inreality,the typeoflovethatisbeingparade dbymanyis,atitsbest,thetypeo flove,whichistypicallytoward afriend,familymember,well-wisher,orsomeotherfriendlyo rneedyacquaintances,andatits worst,itistheerostypeoflove, whichistheeroticorsexuallove thatislust-oftenquicklyfiredupbyanattra ctiveorseductiveappearance(orsomeothersuperficialconsi derations),andrapidlydeflate ButGod,whoisthesourceandi ncarnationofgenuinelove,has revealedtoustheexactcharacteristicsoflovethatwemustpossessifweaaretobeconsideredHisfollowers.Otherwise,ourassertionswouldbebaselessanduntrue.Godwillnottakeintoaccountthecorruptideaoflovethatmenhave.Heisthepersonificationoflove,andHealonecandefineloveforus.In1Corinthians13,Paulassertsthatifweclaimtohavelove,itmustbeagapelove,whichcontainsthefollowingcharacteristics:

(1)Itenduresmuchpain.Itisnotfickleorvolatile.Despitenumerousprovocations,itcontinuestobepeacefulandenjoyable.To saveothersfromperdition,itde cidestosufferwrong.Nomatter howterribleothershavedone,it neverlosescompassionandbec omeshostile.

(2)It'sbenevolent.Itisnotharsh ,butratherkind,gracious,practi cal,enjoyable,andbenevolent. Incontrasttoothertypesoflove, agapeloveconstantlyservesan dgives;itisalwaysshowntooth ersinsteadoftooneself.Givingi sacommonwaytoshowgenero sity,andnooneistoopoortodos o.Everyonecancontributeinso meway— throughmoney,time,talent,pr ayer,etc.—

thoughtheamountandfrequen cymayvary.

(3)Itlacksenvy.Trueloveneve rharborsenvyforthejoyorsucc essofothers.Itdoesn'thaveane nviouslongingforwhatitlacks. (4)Itisn'tinflated.Itdoesnotad vertiseorpromoteitself.Itdoes notexaltitselfforitsabilities,su ccesses,orassets.Itdoesnotma keothersfeellowerorunworth youtofdetestationforthem. (5)Itdoesn'tconductitselfimpr operly.Itdoesnotactinanunco uth,hostile,orimpolitemanner .Itisnotimpatientordesperate.I trespectfullymaintainsitsposit

ionwithoutinfringingonother people'srights.
(6)Itdoesnotlookoutforitself.Itisnotegotistical.Itdoesn'ttrytogetitswayatanycost.Manypeopletodayjustthinkabouttheirownneedsandinterests,focusingonwhattheystandtogainfromanyencounterortransactionratherthanwhattheycanprovidewithoutreceivinganythinginreturn.Theattitudeofloveisnotconstantlyfocusedon"what'sinitforme."
(7)Itresistsbeingprovoked.Itmaintainscontroloveritsanger.Itdoesn'tgeteasilyannoyedorfrustratedbyotherpeople'sflaws.

(8)Ithasnoharmfulthoughts.It doesnotharborsentimentsofh ostility,resentment,orretaliati on.Itdoesn'tcriticizeorpointou tflaws.

(9)Itdoesnottakepleasureininj ustice.Itdoesnottakepleasurei nthefallofothersortakepleasur eininjusticedonetoallegedriva lsorfoes.

(10)Itcarrieseverything.Nom atterhowupsetting,surprising, orhurtful,itdoesn'tgoabouttell ingeveryonewhatitgoesthrou gh.Withoutofferingjustificati onsforimproperbehavior,itac commodatestheshortcomings ofothers.Unquestionably,wro ngiswrong.Makingaccommo dations,however,preventsyou fromcastingthemoffdespiteth eirrepeatedfailures.Itimpliest hatyouareofferingthemaseco ndchance.

(11)Everythingisbelievedbyit .Lovealwaysassumesthebesti nthedeedsandintentionsofoth ers.Truelovedoesn'tproceedw ithunwarrantedsuspicionsand pointlessreservations.

(12)Everythingishoped.Even whensomeonehasgivenupont hemselves,nevergiveuponthe m.

(13)Itwithstandseverything." Allthings"?Doesthisalsoentai lsuffering,inconveniences,an dprivationsforthebenefitofoth ers?Yes!Whataboutthes lights ,insults,backstabbing,malicio ustwistingofourwordstopaint usinanegativelight,payingour gooddeedswithevil,teasing,ta unting,andwillfuldenialofrigh ts?Trueloveforotherswillenab leustoendureitall,Iagree! Nowthatthesourceoflovehasr evealedwhatittrulyentails,let' sstartbyaskingthequestion:do welovethoseweclaimtolove

—

ourpartners,friends,coworker s,neighbors,churchgoers,and nonbelievers— asmuchasweclaimto?Ourlove isnolongerScripturalorChrist-likeifitfallsshortofthesechara cteristics.Thisleadsustoadifferentproblem.WhyisitthatwerequirethisChristlikeloveinourlives?

Chapter4

GodIsLove

Noonecanaccuratelydiscusspurelovewithoutmentioning God.Loveisone'sdedicationtoanotherwithaselfless,devoted, andcharitablemotive.Andnoonecanfullyexhibitsuchaselflessdedicationwithoutreceiving thenatureofGod.Godistheultimateessence,definition,andembodimentoflove.WithoutG od,loveisimpossible.Godisno tself-centered;Hedoesnothoardany thingofvalue.ItisinHisnaturet oalwaysprovideforthebenefit ofallofcreation.

Mentypicallyexpresslovetoot hersforareason(whethertoapp reciate,reciprocate,fulfillares ponsibility,ormerelytoreceive somethinginreturn);inadditio n,suchdisplaysofaffectionaret ypicallynotmadetopeoplewh ohaveseverelyinjuredthem.B utevenwhenwewereleastexpe cting,worthy,orabletorespond ,GodhascontinuedtoshowHisl ovefordisobedientpeople.Thi

sisdemonstratedbythemillion
soflivesaroundtheworldthatc
ontinuetorejectthegospelmes
sage.Evenso,Godstillbestows
blessingsonallpeoplebysendi
ngthesun,rain,andothernatura
lresources.Loveisnotonlyaqu
alityofGod;itiswhoHeis.

Godislove,oncemore.Alltheq
ualitiesoflovearequalitiesofG
od,asextensivelyexemplifiedi
n1Corinthians13.Thus,itfollo
wsthatanythingdevoidoflove
cannotbefromGod.GottistLie
be.Hedoesn'tlookforfaults.He
lacksmalice.Heisn'tevil.Heis
notacarelessperson.Hedoesn't
talkmaliciously.Heisnotretali

ation.Heisnotresentful.Heisn'targuing.Heisn'tdiscord,though.Anywhereandineveryonethatanyofthisispresent,thereisadifferentspiritatworkthatisopposedtotheSpiritofGod.

God'sloveisalsoself-originatingandself-sustaining.Itisbothundeservedandunconditional.Noneofusearneditvialabor.HehadtogosofarastogiveupHisSonasaransom—agiftwedidn'tevenrealizeweneeded—evenwhenwewentastrayandunintentionallysoldourselvestothereignofSatan.Hedidthistod emonstrateHislovefortherebe llious,unworthytraitorswhoha dcampedwiththedevil.Andthi sloveisnotonlyforonerace;itis foreveryracethroughouthistor yandontheentireplanet.

GodsurrenderedHimselftous whenHegaveusHisSonsince HeandtheSonareone(John10: 30).ItmakessensewhytheApo stlequestioned,"Howshallhen otwithhimalsofreelygiveusall things?"Hewhosparednothiso wnSon,butdeliveredhimupfor usall(Romans8:32).Howfarw ouldHenotgotoensureourhap pinessbothhereonearthandint heafterlifeifHecouldhaveHis

Sonenduresuchexcruciatingpain,humiliation,anddeathsimplytofreeusfromourself-inflictedbonds?

Godonlywantsustohavearichandfulllife.tohaveanabundant,fulfillinglifeinHimratherthanalifeofdefeat,cowering,oppression,andbegging.toexperiencethepleasureofsalvationandtheCross'svictory.HedesiresforustobecomeheirstoglorY.IhavelovedyouwitheternaIlove,thusIhaveattractedyouwithlovingkindness,hesays(Jeremiah31:3).

Itwillbefoolishforanyonetoco ntinuetoavoidthiskindoflove, I'msureofit.Reader,acceptHis loveandgiveHimyourheart.A ndifyouhavealreadyacknowle dgedHislove,youbearaheavy burden.JustasGodhaslovedyo u,practicepracticallylovingot hers.Forustobeabletoloveand becomemoreandmorelikeGo d,GodhasgivenusHisSpirit.A saresult,wearewithoutfault,an difwetrulyknowGod,wewilll oveasHeloves.

1.TheloveofGodisinexplicable. Nohumanunderstandingcanu nderstandGod.Godisindefina ble.Weareunabletogiveanindepthdescriptionofwhoheis.H e"residesininaccessiblelight" (1Tim.6:16).God'slovemustal sobeincomprehensible.Event houghwemustbehonestwhile discussinghislove,wewillnev erbeabletounderstanditbecau seitisdivinelove,whichisunlik eourloveinthesamewaythathi sbeingisunlikeours.

2.OnecancomprehendGod'slov e.

WecanaccuratelydescribeGo deventhoughwecannotfullyd efinehiminthesenseofdefinin gwhoheis.Wecanaccomplisht hisbecausehehasshownhimse lftousthroughhisWord,andhe alsouseshisSpirittoopenoureyestothatWord.Whatwiththeheavenlydifference,howisiteven conceivable?Itispossiblebecause Godrevealshimselftousvia thetruthofcreation.Hepicksup thecreationshehasbuiltandtellsusabouthimselfthroughthem.Heisthereforealion,arock,afire,amoth,andevendryrot(checkitup!).

3.Analogieshelpusunderstand God.

IntheBible,Godfrequentlycompareshimselftoothercreated beings,suchaslions.Thisindicatesthatthecharacteristicsheusestocharacterizehimselfaren eitherwhollythesameashimnorwhollydifferentfromhim.Forinstance,heisarockwhilenotbeingbuiltofstone.Whensomeonereferstohimselfasa"rock,"wearenottoattributetohimallthecharacteristicsofarock.Butweshouldn'tassumethatheisdevoidofrocksorthathissurfaceiscompletelyuninterruptedbythem.Heisnotformedofstone,butheissolidandtrustworthy,whichispartofwhatwemeanwhenwesaythatarockisarock.Howisitpossibleforobjectsthatwerecreatedtorepresentgodtousinthisway?Becausehemadethem,itisfeasible.Eachofthethingshecreatedcarriesafaintreflection

ofsomeofhisheavenlyqualitie
sasifhisfingerprintswerelefto
nthem.SinceweconcealGod's
naturalrevelation,ourfallenbr
ainsareunabletoconstructapic
tureofGodfromwhathehascre
ated.However,Godhimselfca
ndescribehimselfinhisinspire
dWord,andthenhemayenlight
enourmindssothatwecancom
prehendandtrustthosedescript
ions.AllofthisistrueofGod'slo
ve:whenwereadthat"Godislo
ve,"wehavesomeideaofwhatl
oveisbasedonthecreationsthat
hehasproduced,buthislovecan
noteverbeidenticaltoanycreat
edlovethatwealreadyknow.

4.ThedepictionsofGodintheBible,particularlythoseofhislove,self-regulate.

Thequestionofhowwecandeterminewhichfeaturesofeachrepresentationof God'sselfweshouldapplytohimandwhichweshouldnotimmediatelyfollow. Howdoweknowthatweshouldnotassumethathislovewouldfailorevenfluctuatelikehumanloveoftendoes?Althoughitmayseemapparenttous,itisonlybecausewehavealreadygainedsomeknowledgeonhowtoproperlyreadtheBible.Whenwepausetoconsiderit,whydon'twedrawthisconclusion?Thisisbec auseotherwaysinwhichGodid entifieshimselfpreventusfrom doingso,suchashisrepeatedcla imstobeacovenant-keepingdeitywhosolemnlysw earstohispeople.TheBibleisab ookthatinterpretsitself;whatit saysinonesectioninstructsuso nhowtoreadanothersection.A self-interpretingmeshofimagesisc reatedbyitsnumerousdepictio nsofGod.Andthatalsocontain simagesofhisaffection.

5.WhenevaluatingGod'slove,w eoftendrawerroneousconclusio ns.

WhenweconsiderGod'sothers
elf-
descriptions,wearefrequently
lessawareofhowthelovelangu
ageistobeapplied.Whensome
onesayssomethinglike,"IfIwe
reaGodoflovethenI...,"thisis
madeextremelyplain.Thelogi
cthatfollowsistypicallynotco
nnectedtohowGodisportraye
dmoregenerallyinScripture.
Whenwedothis,Godessentiall
ytransformsintoagiganticrefl
ectionofourimage—
ashadowcastbehinduswithall
ofourtraitsenlargedandintensi
fied.Whileitmaybeevidenttou
sstraightawaythatGodwillcon
tinuetoloveus,itislessobvioust

ousforsomereasonthathislove differsfromourloveinotherres pects,suchasbeingindependen t,sovereign,unchanging,all-knowing,just,andpassionless(yes,rightlyunderstood).

6.TherestofwhatScriptureteac hesaboutGod'sdivinequalities mustbe"read"inthecontextofG od'slove.

Theideathat"Godislove"isnot ourstotakeupandcarrywherev erweplease.Theremarkmustb eunderstoodinthecontextof1J ohn4,aswellasthelargerconte xtofJohn'swritingsandtheover allcontextofGod'sself-descriptioninallofScripture.In verse10,theimmediatecontextservestoremindusoftherelationshipbetweenloveandpropitiation,whichnecessitatesthatwecomprehendGod'sloveinconjunctionwithhisjusticeandanger.TheultimateapplicationofScripturewillincludeallofGod'sotherqualitiesalongsidehislove.Together,theywillcreateaself-containedmeaningweb.

7.Itisimportantto"interpret"God'slovewithinthecontextofwhattheBiblesaysabouthistriunelife.

John'swritingsalsofrequentlylinkGod'slovetohistriunelifeinalargerframework.Johnenjoy sexpressingthelovebetweentheFatherandtheSonthroughhiswriting.EventheLordJesusisrecordedassayingthattheFatherloveshimbecausehegiveshislifeforothers(John10:17).AllofGod'straitsarethoseoftheoneGodwhoisthreepersons,soloveisnotspecialinthatregard.However,wemustneverlosesightofthetrinitariannatureofGod'slove.

8.UnderstandingGod'sloveinabroadercontexthelpsusavoidmistakes.

Fromatrinitarianperspective,loveiscertainlythemostevidentqualitytoconsider,butwemore easilynoticelovethanunderstanditstheologicalimplicationsofit.Whatadifferenceitwillmake,forinstance,ifweremember thattheFather'sloveforhisSonandhissubsequentdesiretoseetheSonrespectedformthefoundationofGod'slove(John5:22–23).Then,wewillunderstandthatsinthatdispleasesGodisanoffenseagainsttheverynatureofhisloveandnotconcludefromthefactthat"Godislove"thathereadilyoverlooksevil.God'sangertowardsinnerswillemanatefromhisloveforhisSon.TheonlywaywecanavoidmisinterpretingGod'slovebyusingournaturalthinkingasthebackdropfori nterpretationisifwereadthelov eofGodinthisway.

9.Recognizingthevariousexpres sionsofGod'sloveenablesustogr aspitsimmeasurablescope. Itisnotanabstractexerciseofint erestonlytoobscurantistsyste matictheologiansthattheconte mplationofGod'sloveinitspro perscripturalsettingsiswarran ted.Itcouldbesimplertojustthi nk,"Godislove,"andthenfillth atthoughtwithwhateverideasc ometomind.Toletourbrainscr eateourtheologyratherthanput tingthemthroughtherigorouss tudyofGod'sself-

revelationintheBiblecertainly involveslessmentalwork.Buti ntheend,Icanneverbesatisfied withagodwhoisnothingmoret hanamanifestationofmythoug hts.Similartotheologicalsolita ryconfinement,awfulnarcissis ticsolipsism,andultimatelyas ortofself-
worshippingidolatrysimilarto hellitself,worshipingsuchadei tywouldbelikebeingconfinedt oaroomwithonlymyselfasaco mpany.Onthispath,thereisonl ypainfuldisappointment;there isnosatisfaction.Oursoulswill findpeaceincontemplatingGo d'sauthoritativeself-
revelationinitswhole;restthat

comesfromdiscoveringinhim onewhogreatlyexceedsourme agerfinitudeandwhosepleasur esareunending.

10.WhenwefullyexperienceGo d'slove,wealwaysrespondwithl ove.

ItisneveranendinitselftoreflectondivineloveinitsbiblicalfullIness.OurrestinGodneverfinds satisfactioninourselves;rather ,italwaysdrawsusawayfromo urselvesandtowardGodandot hers.Bothlearningaboutandpr acticingGod'slovearenecessar y.God'sloveforusproduceslov einusforbothhimandforothers .IfwetrulybelievewhattheBibl esaysaboutlove,itwilldwellin usandwillnotleaveuswhenwe useactsofgracetomakeonlypa ssingreferencestotheinfinitel oveofGodthatappearedtoothe rsinourownlives. "Godislove;hewhoabidesinlo veabidesinGod,andGodinhim ,"theBiblesays(1John4:16)

Chapter5

LivingAndLovingWith Wisdom

ExemplaryApplication

Now,let'sseehowJesusHimsel fappliedthistoHispersonallife .InJohn18:22-

23,wearetold,"Andwhenhehadthusspoken,oneoftheofficerswhichstoodbystruckJesuswiththepalmofhishand,saying,Answerestthouthehighpriestso?Jesusansweredhim,IfIhavespokenevil,bearwitnessoftheevil:butifwell,whysmitestthoume?"AtHistrial,JesushadjustaddressedthehighpriestasformallyandgraciouslyasHecould.Hisresponsedidn'tmerittheslapHegotfromoneoftheofficersstandingclosetoHim.Now,Hecouldhavejustsaid,"ThisisthemomenttopracticewhatIhavepreached.Youslappedmeontherightcheek;hitmeontheleftalso."ButHedidn'tgivethecopHi sothersidetohit.Instead,Hemadehimrecognizethathisbehaviorwasneitherlawfulnorreasonable.ThatshowsusthatHedoesn'twantustotakeliterallythedirectionsintheversesofourconcentration.

Letmedigressalittle,IindicatedbeforethattograspGod'swordandproperlyapplyit,youneedtheSpiritofChrist,themindofChrist,theloveofChrist,thelifeofChrist,andthewisdomofChrist.Romans8:9states,"Butyouarenotinthebody,butintheSpiritifsobethattheSpiritofGoddwellsinyou.NowifanyonehasnottheSailofChrist,heisnoneofhis."Thismeansthatstartswith,in dividualswhoarenotbornagaindonothavetheSpiritofChristandconsequentlycannotinterprettheversesunderdiscussionforus.So,don'tallowsomeonearoundyoutojustpullupaverseofthescriptureoutofcontextandproceedtosay"Hey!LetmetellyouwhatJesussaid.."YouwillasktheguytoholdhispeacebecauseheneedstheSpiritofChristtobeabletointerprettheScriptureofChrist.

ExemptedAreas

Sometimes,tocomprehendwhatsomethingis,itisimportanttostudywhatitisnot.SimplyImeanthatevaluatingaspectsoflife, situations,andrelationshipsinwhichthesewords,notablyverse39,donotapplycanmakeunderstandingthemaloteasier.First,JesuswasnottalkingabouttherelationshipbetweenakingandhissubjectHewasn'tinstructingthekingtoturntheothercheekifheissmittenbyhissubject.No,suchasubjectshouldbesubjectedtolawfulsanctions.Secondly,Hewasn'ttalkingabouttherelationshipbetweenparentsandtheirchildren.Hewasnotsuggestingifyourchildsmitesyouononecheek,turntohimtheotherlikewise.Hewasn'tsuggestingifyouryoungsterdisregardsanddisobeysyou,reasonwithh imandcondonehisattitude,No. Onthecontrary,ifyourchilddo essomethingheshouldbechast isedappropriatelyandmadetor ecognizethenecessitytohonor hisparents.Youshouldn'tthusl istentoarebelliouschildwhoco mplains,"Whyareyoupunishi ngme?Doesn'tGod'swordindi cateyoushouldnotresistevil?" Thirdly,thesetofinstructionsis notapplicabletotheinteraction betweenateacherandhisstude nts.Imagineateacherwhosepu pilcontinuestomisbehavedesp iterepeatedwarnings.Whatdo youbelieveshouldbetheteache r'sanswerYouandIknowquite wellthatthatteacherwouldnot

dowelltooverlookthestudent's
behavior.Fourthly,thisisnotap
plicabletoamasterandhisdisci
ple.JesusChristhasHisdiscipl
es,twelveofthem.AndHelove
dthemdearly.Butitdidn'tmean
thatanyofthemcoulddoorsay
whateverhelikedaroundHim.
Ononeoccasion,Petertriedtoc
ontradictHimwhenHestated,"
Beitfarfromthee,Lord:thissha
llnotbeuntothee."Jesus'respo
nsetothatwasnotpatronizing.
HesternlyrebukedPetersaying
,"Gettheebehindme,Satan"(
Matthew16:22-
23).(Matthew16:22-23).
Lastly,thisdoesnotapplytoane
mployerandhisemployee.Ifan

employeeforanyreasondecide stobecontinuouslyirresponsib le,reckless,bad-mannered,andprofessional,w hatisexpectedisthatheshouldb ewarned,andifthatdoesn'twor k,potentiallydismissed.Itwill beagrossmisreadingoftheScri pturetoinformsuchanemploye r,"AreyounotaChristian?DidJ esusnotsaythatifsomebodysm itesyouontherightcheek,turnt ohimtheotheralso?"

Letmealsobringyourattention toverse40ofourtext.

Andifanymanshallsuetheebef orethelaw,andtakeawaythycl othing,lethimhavethycloaklik ewise."Onethingyoumusthav einthebackofyourmindwhenyoureadthisisthatJesuswasn'treferringtobelievers.Abelieverwillnottakeanotherbelievertothelegalcourt.God'swordclearlyforbidsthis(See1Corinthians6:1-7).(See1Corinthians6:1-7).Christwasactuallyreferringtoacircumstancewhereanunbelieverrefusestobepersuadedandinsistsontakingabelievertocourt.WhattheLordencouragesisthatasapeace-lovingchildofGodwhohasnothingdarktohide,thebelievershouldnothesitatetogoaheadandhavethesituationsettledbeforetheauthorities.(See1Peter2:13-15).

ExpectedAttitude

NowthatwehavelearnedfromtheexampleofChristthatHedidn'tmeanforustofollowliterallythesetofinstructionsinourtext,andwehavealsoexploredwhattheinstructionsdonotmean,thequestionweneedtoaskourselvesiswhatmessageisinitforusasChristianstoday?OrisChristtellingustobecomeintolerant,"nononsense",spitefulpeople?No,it'squitethecontraryHewantsustobepeopleoftheloveofmercyandcompassionTheideaofhighlightingandexplainingthetextisbasicallytoassistustohaveabetterknowledgeofwhatthe

Lordgenuinelyasksofus,withoutgettingconfusedordeceivedbytheignorant.

So,whatisthisexpectation?ThefirstsectionofMatthew5.39says,"ButIsayuntoyou..."(Whatanauthority!Here,Christsaysitdoesn'tmatterwhatyouhavelearnedinthepast.Itdoesn'tmatterwhathumanrightscampaignersthink.Itdoesn'tmatterwhatyourownfeelingorprincipleisForgeteverythingandtaketothis)."ButIsayuntoyouthatyeresistnotevil..."Don'tbesorepelledandoffendedbywrongsdonetoyouthatyoubecomesobitterandseektoretaliate.Ifsomeonetreatsyouharshly,don'thitback.Y oumaycalmlymaketheperson knowyou'reupset,outraged,or saddened.Butdonotretaliate.T hat'swhatJesusmeantwhenHe saidnottoopposeevil. Ofcourse,physicallyspeaking ,itmightbeatremendouslytoug honetojustfoldyourarmsandle tsomeoneinfringeonyourright s,swindleyouortakewhatispro perlyyours.Ittakesgrace,ittak esenormousself-controltobeabletostillloveand treatsuchanindividualgraciou sly.Butthisisoneofthecardinal proofsofactualconversion.Thi siswhatdividesaChristianfro maheathen.

TheLordevengoesfurthertoad d,"Thereforeifthyenemyhung erfeedshim...becauseinthusdo ingthoushaltheapcoalsoffireo nhishead.Benotovercomeofe vil,butovercomeevilwithgood "(Romans12:20- 21).(Romans12:20- 21).Didyouseethat?Feedyour opponentifheishungry.Whata command!Shouldn'tyoufeelr elievedthatyouroppressorishu ngry?Afterall,ifheishungryth atmeansthathewillnothavethe strengthtoattackyouagain.Wh athappenswhenheregainsstre ngth?Whatifheintendstohurty ouagain?Still,Godwhoseesall thingsandiswiserthanall,says, "Feedhim."

Sure,thereasonablemindmay deemthisexceedinglysilly.Bu tGodinHiswisdombelievesth atyouruniqueactofcompassio niswhatwillbreakthatguydow nandchangehishearttoGod.If yourenemyisneedy,helphim. Don'tdelightoverhissorrow.D on'tconsideritasGod'swayofp unishinghim.Youneverknow howmanyindividualsyoucand rawtoGodbythisdoing.

Onceagain,let'srememberthat itwillbedifficulttolovetheway Godexpectsusto,withoutthea ppropriateknowledgeofHisw ord;itwillbefarfrompossibleto loveothersasyououghttoifyoudonothavethementalityofChrist.

LetmesumitallupbysayingthatlikeChrist,ourlives(speech,action,character)shouldnotcontradictwhatwepreach.Ifyou'reasincerebeliever,thendon'tallowyourlifestyletoconfuseyourhearers.AsforChrist,weonlyhavetolookatthewayHelivedtocomprehendplainlywhatHetaught.Howaboutyou?DoyouloveTheLord?AreyoucontinuallyabidinginthatLove?Areyouspreadingthatlovearound?IfyoureallyareabidingintheloveofChrist,thenyoumustwalkpreci

selyasHewalked(1John2:6).(
1John2:6).

Chapter6

Nopriceistoohigh

Akidwhosincerelyneedstopro gresstothenextlevelacademic allywouldtellyouthatthere'sre allynopricetoohighforachieve ment.Aguyorwomanwhodesp eratelywantstoearntheloveofa notherwillgotolengthsinconc eivabletoattainthis.Whatthisr eallymeansisthatnopricemay betooexpensivetopayfortruel ove.

Love,whichistheverycharacte rofGod,ismoreoftenthannote xpensive.ForGodtoshowusho wmuchHelovesus,He"spared nothisownSon"(Romans8:32).(Romans8:32).OurloveforG odalsoshouldurgeustotellothe rsofHisgreatsacrifice,justaso urloveforothersandtheirnever dyingsoulswillcompelustowa rnthemofthedangerofrejectin gGod'slove.

GodinHisdivinitymakesthesu nriseuponallandlikewisesend stheraindownonall,includingt hosewhoresistHim.HesentHi sonlySonforuswhilewewerey etinoursins(Romans5:8).(Ro mans5:8).Similarly,asachildo fGod,youareexpectedtolovee verybody,evenyouradversari es,nomatterhowunlovableand hostiletheyare.Andthebestma nifestationofthisloveistoinfor mthemofthelovethatledChrist todieahorribledeathfortheirsa ke.

WecanreachallkindsofindividualsforChristandwemustNomattertheriskorperilcost.timeanddevotion,wemustreachouttosoulsinloveitmaytaketimebeforetheyrespondtoyoubutthat'spartofthepriceyoumustpay,AndwillingnesstopaythispriceisanindicationofyourdeeploveforGodandrealaffectionfortheperishing.

Ifhowever,youhavenotexperiencedtheloveofGod,realizethatitwillbeimpossibleforyoutobedrivenbythislove.Topaythepriceforlove,youmustfirstcomeintoanintimateconnectionwithGod.Andsecondly,youalsoneedyourheartsanctifiedfor ittobefilledwiththeGodsortofl ove.See,evangelismthatdoesn 'tspringfromaheartfulloflove willonlyamounttoanemptypr oclamationbecausethemessag eyouractiondeliverstothoseyo uareseekingtoreachissometi mesmoreimportantthanthatof yourvoice.Prayerisanotherpri cetopayinyoureffortofreachin gouttolostpeoplearoundyouT heroleofprayerinsoul-winningcannotbeoveremphas izedYouneedtopraythattheHo lySpiritwillsoftentheirheartsi nreadinessfortheWordandyo ualsopraytobringintosubjecti oneveryspiritincitingthemaga instthegospel.Moreover,whe nyouareinconstantconnectionwithGod,yougettoknowHimmore,andthemoreofHimyouknow.themoreyourloveforHimrises.AndthemoreyourloveforHim,themoreyouwanttoconductserviceforHim.

ThispricewearetalkingabouthasbeenpaidbymanyinthepastThoughsomeofthesepeoplearenolongeralivetheirfruitsarestillfloweringintheirthousandsJimElliotandNateSaintwereslaughteredbyasavagetribetheyweretryingtoevangelizeinEcuadorYearslater,theirwiveswentbackthere,forgivenandlovedtheirhusband'smurderersandstillproceededtosharethegosp elofChristlivingamongthem. Theoutcomeswereastounding !AdoniramandAnnJudsonand anendlesshostofotherslikewis epaidthepricewiththeirbloodo utofpureloveforGodandtheso ulsofmen.Thoughdeceased.th eirworksstillspeakandmanyar edevotingtheirlivestoJesusall becauseoftheirwitnessWhata boutApostlePaulPeter,James, andotherearlyapostlesofChris twhoriskedtheirlivessothegos pelwouldreachtheextremities oftheearth?

Nowit'syourtime,readerWhat areyouwillingtogiveupforthel oveofChrist?Christpaidtheult imatepriceoflovebydyingtopr ocureyoursalvationAndyoum ustgotowhateverlengthtospre adthenewsofHissacrificialdea thandwhatitbrings- peacewithGodandlifeforever Salvationcomeswithoutapric etag,butthecalltodiscipleshipi sacostlyone.itmaycostyouyou rbloodSinceGoddidn'tthinkan ypricetooexpensivetopayfory ourredemption,youshouldcon sidernopricetoohightoshareH isloveandrescueothersontheb rinkofthefurnaceofhell. Godwillundoubtedlyrewards oulwinnerswhoneverconsider anypaymenttooexpensivefort henever- dyingsoulsofmen.Hewillneve roweanyman.Theseeminglyhefty priceyouhavetopaytodayisnothingcomparedtothegrandeurandrecompenseyouwillbegrantedattheendoftimeAstheScriptureassures"AndtheythatbewiseshallshineasthebrightnessofthefirmamentandtheythatturnmanytorighteousnessasthestarsforeverandeverDaniel12:3)

Chapter7

Bestoffriends

OnlyGodknewhowlongtitleJa meshadbeenatthedoorwatchi ngHisnanny,Betty,whohadbe enmonitoringhimforclosetoth reeminutes,decidedtocomecl oseenoughtodiscoverwhathel dheryoungchildsoenthralled. Beforeshecouldreachwhereh estood,however,heswungaro undShehaddefinitelystartledh im.Thathadn'tbeenheraim.Bu tshedidn'thavecausetofear.Th eboywasfineAtleastthelooko nhisfaceinformedherthatwhat everitwashehadbeenstaringat madehimincrediblyhappy.He brimmedfromeartoear.

Thinkingabouttheoccurrence manyyearslater,JamesSmiths miledtohimself.Hehadlikedo bservinghisparentsasachild. Whenevertheygotbackfromw orkthey'dspendsometimeinth egarage,talkingliketheyhadn'treturnedfromworkinthesamecar.Hewatchedthematthedinning-table.Thewayhismumwouldblushattheslightestpraisefromdaddyoverthecuisine.Whenevertheytookwalks,daddyalwayshuggedmamaeversoprotectivelyTheduowerejustsointothemselvesHerecallsaskinghisdadwhohisbestfriendwasHegrinnedwhendadhadtoldhimthathisbestbuddywashismum.Truly,hisparentswerebestfriends.GrowingupinahomewheretherewassomuchloveandwhereGoddominatedhelpedJamesgrowintoaGod-fearing,God-honouring,andlovingguy.Heg otemployedpromptlyfollowin ghisundergraduateeducationa ndsoonrealizedthenecessityto getmarriedandsettledown.Ha vingobservedhisparentsfromt hetimehewasachildtillhereac hedtheage,hevowedtosettledo wnwithsomeonehehadknown closelyrightfrominfancysotha ttheytoomightenjoythesameb ondhisparentshad.Unfortunat ely,theladyhehadinmindwant ednothingmorethanbeingame re\sacquaintance.

Heartbroken,heconfidedinhis father.whocounseledhimthatt hebestthingtodowastalktoGo daboutwhotomarryandallow

Himtodeterminewhowasbestf orhim.Hisfathertoldhimthath eandhismotherhadn'tbeenbest offriendsbeforetheygotmarrie d.Theyhadformedtheirbondo vertheyearsintheirmarriage.H eoriginallyknewheratschool. Theyhadbeeninthesamefacult yandhadhadonlyveryminimal meetings.Theyhadmadefrien dsduringtheircompulsoryone - yearservice,andayearafterthe servicetheyweremarried.Itwa sfromthattimetheybeganform ingalong-lastingfriendship.

Thefactthathisparentsbuiltthe irownfriendshipsinmarriageg

aveJamesarenewedoptimismthathecouldstillbebestoffriendswithhisbride.HeedinghisFather'ssuggestion,hedecidedtotrytalkingtoGodabouttheppersontogetmarriedto.Shortlyafterhestartedpraying,hemetthisladyatayouthcampmeeting,andinstantlyheknewshewashiswife.TheyhadspentafewsecondschattingatthemeetingandithadseemedNDSasthoughtheyhadknowneachotherforalifetime.Followingtheprocedureinhischurch,JameswassoonmarriedtothecharmingJanetBright.Indeed,theirsseemedliketheclassicmarriagemadeinparadise.Witheachpassingday,theywit nessedhowmuchtheyhadfalleninloveandhowprofoundlytheirlovedeepened.Youcouldhardlycapturethemontheirown. Everyoneattheirlocalassemblyknewthe Smithsasinseparable.couple.Boththemarriedandthesingleswantedtobearoundthemsincetheirunionepitomizedtruefriendship.

Janet,whenaskedbyotherwomentodescribeherhusband,statedthebestwayshecoulddescribehimwasasherbestfriend.The secrettothesuccessoftheirrelationshipwasmostlyGod.TheyaccordedHimHisappropriatepositionintheirownlifeandhomeaswell.Asawoman,shehadta kentimetostudyherhusbandto knowwhatthelovedandhated,a ndasaresult,therewaslesstensi onbetweenthem.Wheneverth eydidhavemomentsofmisund erstanding,theyneverallowedt histopersist.Theyalwaysresol vedeveryquarrelovermeals.T heyhadmadeadecisionnevert ocarryanyoffensetobed.Andt hishaspaidoffforthemoverthe years.

FosteringIntimacy

Loveisthecoreofanymeaningf ulrelationship,includingmarri age.Everyotherfacetofmarria gelifeiscenteredonthisextrem elyvitalfactor.Now,aseverytr uemarriageisbuiltonlove,itmustalsocontinueinloveforitspurposetobecompleted. Whereasloveissupposedtobeabstractsyntactically,trueloveissubstantial,palpable,tangible,andinfluential;itisfeltwhencommunicatednotjustinwords,butthroughpracticalandconstructiveacts.Itisnotpossibletobearoundthephysicalfireandnotfeeltheheat,exceptifitismanufacturedormake-believe.Similarly,whentrueloveflourishesathome,thefruitsarethereforalltoseeandenjoy. Loveisthecordthatlinksthemarriagerelationshiptogetherandstopsitfromunraveling.Itislov ethatmakesmarriageblossom. Andinthistopicoflove,thewomanisreallycrucial.Asawife,theatmosphereinandaroundthehomeismostlysetbyher.Itisnecessarythereforethatshebeclothedwithloveandexudeloveallaroundher.Sheisnotonlyorderedtoloveherhusbandandteachotherwomentolovetheirhusbandsaswell,butsheisalsoreallyenabledtoloveandclingtoherhusbandbytheLordGodAlmightyHimself,andthatrightatthebeginning.directlyafterthefall(Genesis3:16;Ephesians5:24:Titus2:4).(Genesis3:16;Ephesians5:24:Titus2:4).

TheChristianwomanwhoprof esseslovetoherhusbandconse quentlymustdemonstrateitinp racticalterms.Shemustrelatew ithherhusbandwithlove respec t,devotion,andsacrificialcom mitment.Shemustcherishherh usbandandcontinuallythankG odfortheblessingofmarryingh im.Atypicalerrormanywome nmakeistocomparetheirhusba ndswithotherwomen'shusban dsandtrytomoldormoldhimint otheimageoftheiridealman.T hisoughtnottobe.FortheChrist ianwoman,herspouseisthebes tandreallyincomparable.Ifshe hassoughtGod'sperfectwillfor aspouse,shealreadyunderstan dsthatGodhasgivenherjusttha t;andassuch,shemustrelatewit hherhusbandinlove,inappreci ationofthismagnificentgift.Sh emustloveherhusbandforwho heisandnotforwhomheisnot.S hemustrememberthatthereca nnotbeanyexactpersonlikehi mandthathewasspecificallyin tendedforhertoadoreandtoche rish...tilldeathdothempart!

If,asaChristianwife,youperce iveyourhusbandlikethis,itwill besimpleforyoutorelatewithh immoreintimately,youwillbe abletoshareandenjoyprivatem omentstogetherthatyoucan,an dmust,neversharewithanyoth erperson.Forone,thetwoofyo umustbeemotionallylinkedtoeachother;butyouasawifemustbeparticularlyattachedtoyourhusbandifyouwantyourmarriagetoblossomasGodcreatedittobe.Youmustneverdistanceyourselvesfromhim.Youmustgotogether,flowtogether,growandglowtogether.Shareinterestsandactivitiestogetherasmuchaspossibleanddevelopyourconnectionandfriendshiptogetherastheyearsgoby.Whenthishappens,youwillnoticethatyoualwaysrevelinandseekeachother'scompanionship,somuchsothattemporaryseparationduetosomeexpediencyistypicalwithmuchreluctance.

Suchisthekindoflovethatmustbondhusbandandwifetogetherinanideal Christianfamilyandthat'sGod'srequirementforeverywoman:toloveandtodoteonherhusband.Thislovedevelopsthemutualandharmoniousrelationshipbetweenthehusbandandthewife;itisthelovethatrespectseachother'spersonalityandpeculiarityanddoesnotexposetheotherunnecessarily;itisthekindoflovethathidesthemultitudeofsins.Manoah'swifedisplayedthiskindoflovewhensheallayedthedreadofManoahwhichheexpressedwhenhesuddenlyfoundtheyhadbeenspeakingwithanangel.Manoahfeltth atthissignifieddoomforthem, butthewomanwiselyyettenderlyallayedherhusband'sconcerns(Judges13:21-23).(Judges13:21-23).Shedidn'tberatehimfornotdisplayingenoughfaith,courage,ordiscernment.Whenyouloveyourhusband,youwouldnotwanthimtosimplyfeelembarrassedofhimself,letalonemakehimanobjectofmockerywhetheryouarealonebyyourselvesorwithanotherperson.Youwillneverdespisehimeveninyourheartas Michaldid,ifyousincerelylovehim,nomatterhowcrudehehasbehaved(2Samuel6:14-23).(2Samuel6:14-

23).Asamatterofprinciple,youmustbeyourhusband'sconfidant;hemustbefreetoletyouintohisinnermostbeing,hisdeepestworries,concerns,hisactsandinactions,wrong-doings,andblunders.Hemustbefreetocommunicatewithyouunreservedly;youaretheclosesttohim,andhemustbeyourdearesttooineverysenseoftheword.Givehimyourfaithfulsupportandassurance;lethimknowyouarehisnumberonefan,anytime,anyday.

Bythesametoken,yourhusbandmustbeyourbestfriend;heisthepersonwithwhomyoumustr evealyourdeepestsecrets,thin gsyouwillneverdiscusswithan ybody.Hemustknowyouthrou ghandthrough;thatimpliesthe reisnoelementofyourlifethaty ouarepurposelyhidingfromhi m.Isaiah58:7warnsusnottohid efromourownbodies.Thisdoe snotmakeanysenseatall;asyou cannotpossiblyhidefromyour self!"...becausetwo,declaresh e,shallbeoneflesh"(1Corinthi ans6:16).(1Corinthians6:16).

FacingIssues

Realistically,foracoupletobet hegreatestoffriendsdoesnotne cessarilymeanthattheywillal waysunderstandeachotherora lwaysagreeoneverything.No. Therewillundoubtedlybeperi odsofconflict.Butinatrulylovi ngrelationship,thepair,beingb estoffriends,willargueinanacc eptablemanner.Thelovebetwe enadotingpairencouragesthe mtotalkthingsover,esteeming eachothergreaterthanthemsel ves.Noonetriestoclaimasuper iorargumentinthematterthatc omesup,buteachallowsthespir itoflovetotriumphandwinthed ay.Andifthetopicistoothornyt obesolvedthroughdialogue,th eyutilizetheweaponofprayero fagreement.Andbecausethey walkinlove,theyretainnounfo rgivingspiritagainsteachother

,nomattertheoffense.Eachrela
teswiththeotherandmemberso
fthefamilywithbowelsoflove
withitscomponentsmercy.kin
dness,sensitivity,andcompass
ion(Colossians3:12-
14).(Colossians3:12-14).
Coupleswhohavemadealifeti
mecommitmenttobuildingup
eachotherneverallowtheirdiff
erencestodegradeintofuriousf
ightingortodevelopawallofse
parationbetweenthem.Instead
,theyexploitthoseareasofdiffe
rencestoenhanceandspicethei
rconnectionandcomplemente
achother.Theyattempttogetint
otheworldofeachotherandapp
reciateeachother'sspecificinte

rests,eventhoughitmaynotbee njoyableinitially. Forinstance,whileyouasawife maynothavealltheknowledge orexpertiseinyourhusband'sh obbyorchosencareer,someoft hethingshediscusseshisintere stsmightevenbeaboveyourhe ad,yetyourloveforhimwillco mpelyoutopayattentiontohim ashediscussesthedetailsofhis workandlife- passionswithyou.Youmustbei ntelligentsoastobeabletooffer alittleoratstasksomeusefulqu estions.Youmaynottrulyneedt heinformationheprovidestoy ou,butyoumustlistenandpayra ptattention.Itdoesnobodyany goodwhenyouremaindistant,andapatheticorprovidepressurethathisofficediscussionisaboretoyouandthathewouldleavediscussionconcerninghisoffice.Mennormallyarenotinclinedtomuchtalking;thuswhenyourhusbandstartsconversingwithyouonanyissue,youmustrecognizeitasaprivilegeandgivehimthelisteningear.

Knowthatanotherwatchwordforthetrulyvirtuousladyisindustry.AsreportedinProverbs31:13,herloveforher □.mmmhouseholdwillmakeherseekwoolandflaxandworkfreelywithherhands.Whateversshedoesforherfamilyisnotbyco mpulsionbutfromalovingand eagerheart. Especially,inthesetimesofeco nomicdownturn,asavirtuous woman,youmustbeaneconom istintheareaofseekingavenues tospendlessonfoodandothern ecessitiesasyoudeliberatelylo okoutformarketswherefoodst uffscanbeboughtcheapersoth atsomemoneycanbesavedtom eetotherfamilypressingneeds. Itisawell-knowntruththatcertainfoodite mscanbeacquiredcheaperinse lectmarketsinruralareas.You willtakeadvantageofsuchposs ibilitiesratherthanwhiningand lamentingoverseeminginadeq uacies.Theloveyouhaveforyourfamilywillcompelyouasmuchaspossibletoaddresstherequirementsofyourhouseholdwhilesuchmembersareevensleepingcomfortablyintheearlymornings(asevidencedintheexampleofthebiblicalvirtuouswomanProverbs31:15).(asseenintheexampleofthebiblicalvirtuouswomanProverbs31:15). Note,though,thatthiskindoflovedoesn'tjusthappen.Inreality,itwillseemabsolutelyimpossibleandirrational,ifawomanstilllivesinthefleshandhasnotbeenregeneratedbythebloodoftheLamb.Thenaturalwomanisvicious,notvirtuous;shecannotlo veorsubmittoherhusbandaspr escribedbyGod."Becausethec arnalmindishostilityagainstG od:foritisnotsubjecttothelawo fGod,neitherindeedcanbe.Sot hentheythatareinthefleshcann otpleaseGod(Romans8:7- 8).(Romans8:7- 8).Butwhenshebecomesborn oftheSpiritofGod,shewillnolo ngermanifesttheactsofthefles h,sincethegraceforvirtuousliv ingwillhavebeengrantedtoher .

FortifyingInterestsThereisno doubtthatawomannaturallyin vestsalargeamountoftimeinhe rchildrenasshecaresforthema ndseesthemgrow.Shekeepslo

vingthemandtendingtotheme
venwhentheyhavegrownadult
sandhavestartedestablishingt
heirownfamilies.However,th
etiebetweenherandherhusban
dmustbestrongerthanthatwhi
chexistsbetweenherandherchi
ldren.WhattheScriptureadvis
esisforthemantoleavehisfathe
randhismotherandcleavetoget
herwithhiswifesothattheycou
ldweaveintooneandremainto
getherforever.Whereasthechi
ldrenarenottoremainwiththeir
parentsforever,theymustleave
themonedayandcreatetheirow
nfamilies.Itisthislovebetween
thehusbandandwifethatwillsu
staintheмandenablethemtow

eatherthestormsoflifetogether ,evenwhenthechildrenhavelef thomeandwhenoldagecreepsi n.

Thisiswhatmakestrueloveobv ious.Itisperpetuallyconstant.I tdoesnotvarywithtimeortide. Counterfeitlove(basedonbeau tyandothershallowfactors)wil lfadeawaywithtime,itcannotr esistlife'svicissitudesYoumus tbevigilantthereforeincreatin gandfosteringdeep,real,andin tenseloveforyourspousesotha teveninthefaceofanyadversity ,youmaydeepenintimacyandp assioninyourmarriage.Facesu chproblemswithkindnessands tayafriendreallytoyourhusban d.Youmustthencontinuetocon versetogether,fellowshiptoge therspendspecialtimetogether ,andmakeouttimetobealoneto gethereitheroutsideorwithint hehome.Fromtimetotime,sin gtogether,laughtogether,andi fithappens,sharethepaintoget her,shareyourlivestogetheran dmultiplyyourdelighttogether !

Asyouprayerfullywalkinlove andinthemethodindicatedinth iswrite- up,withGodonyourside,youw illhaveyouprosperousmarriag einJesus'name.Makeyourhus bandyourbestfriendandlethim beyourlover.Thatiswhenboth

ofhomechasetenthousand.Lo
veisalifeventureanditistreme
ndouslyrewarding.Allowthel
oveofGodtogovernyourheart
andhousehold.

Chapter8

Giveitallittakes

FromaccountsintheBibleasw ellasmanyyearsofexperiencea sapreacher,Ihavediscoveredt hatthereisatendencytomisund erstandandmisinterprethewo rdofGodifyoudon'tpossessthe Spiritthemind,andthewisdom ofChristReadingfromMatthe w5.38-
42,youwilldiscoverasetofinst ructionsthatChristgaveasHed eliveredHissermononthemou nt"Yehaveheardthatithathbee nsaid.Aneyeforaneye,andato othforatooth:ButIsayuntoyou

,Thatyeresistnotevil:butwhos oevershallsmitetheeonthyrig htcheek,turntohimtheotherals o.Andifanymanwillsuetheeatt helaw,andtakeawaythycoat,le thimhavethycloakalso.Andw hosoevershallcompeltheetog oamile,gowithhimtwain.Give tohimthatasketh thee,andfrom himthatwouldborrowoftheetu rnnotthouaway."

Theseversesarelargelymisun derstoodandthus,misappliedb ymanyThePhariseesinChrist' sday,forinstance,misinterpret edtheruleinDeuteronomy19:2 1tomeanthattheycouldtakeve ngeanceonanyonewhooffend edthem."Andthineeyeshallno tpity;butlifeshallgoforlife,eyeforaneye,toothfortooth,handforhand,footforfoot."Butifyoureadfromverse16ofthatchapteryouwilldiscoverthattherulewasactuallygivenbyGodtotheleadersoftheIsraelitestosettledisputesamongthem.WhatwassupposedtobeamethodofenforcingjusticeforthejudgeslaterbecameatoolofvengeanceinthehandsofthePharisees.

Inabidtocorrectthismisinterpretation,JesussaidinMatthew5:38-39,"Yehaveheardthatithathbeensaid,Aneyeforaneye,andatoothforatooth:ButIsayuntoyou,Thatyeresistnotevil:but,wh

osoevershallsmitetheeonthyri ghtcheek,turntohimtheotheral so.Butthenagain,eventhisismi sunderstoodbymanybelievers today.Peoplehavereaddiffere ntmeaningsintothis.Incorrectl yinterpretingwhatChristsaidf romverses38- 42youmustaskyourselfcertain questions.One,whatexactlyw asHeimplying?Two,howdid HeapplythistoHispersonallife ?Three,whatunderstandingdi dChrist'sdiscipleshaveofthis? Andfour,howdoesthisapplyto mpersonallife?
Tobeginwith,whatdidJesusm eanwhenHesaidifyouareslapp edononecheek,turntheotheral

so;ifyourcoatistakenawayfro
myou,giveawayyourcloakas
well;ifyouarecompelledtogoa
milewithsomeone,goanextra
mileandsoon?WasJesusactua
llysayingthattheseinstruction
sbetakenliterally?Thisiswhat
youmustfindoutinordertound
erstandtheseandbylookingatt
heimplicationoftakingthesein
structionsliterally.If,forinstan
ce,youweretoliterallytake"res
istnotevil:butwhosoevershall
smitetheeonthyrightcheek,tur
ntohimtheotheralso"itmeanst
hatyoureardrumswillsoonbur
stopen.Imaginewhatdamagec
ancometoyoureardrumsifyou

arecontinuallybeingslappedbyeverybody. Againtotake"Andifanymanwillsuetheeatthelaw,andtakeawaythycoat,lethimhavethyclokealso"literally,youwouldsoonbecomeafoot-matforeveryonetotrampleupon.Ifyouwerealsotoliterallytake"Andwhosoevershallcompeltheetogoamile,gowithhimtwain"theimplicationwouldbethatyouwillsoonwearoutfromtoomuchlabor.Moreso,ifyouweretotake"Givetohimthatasketh thee,andfromhimthatwouldborrowoftheeturnnotthouaway"literally,itimpliesthatyouwouldsoongobankrupt.Ifpeoplek newthatyoucouldneversaynot otheirrequestformoneytheyw ouldsoonmilkyoutothelastpe nnyandprobablyputyouindebt .

RealitiesofOurResponsibility

GodinHisinfinitewisdomhasg ivenmanycounselsanddirecti onsintheBibletoadviseuspare ntsonraisingdelightsomechild ren.Incidentally,oursisthebest ofallcareersbecauseitisGod-ordained.Anaccountofourste wardshiphastobegiventoGod sometimes.Realizingthisshou ldmakeusgivekidtraininginw hateveritrequires.Careerambi tions,commercialneeds,churchactivities,socialengagements,oranyothercommitmentmustnotimpedeusfromperformingitefficiently.

Besides,ofallourearthlygoods,theonlyonesthatwilllastforalleternityareouroffspring.So,whynotgiveineverythingtoensurethattheyarewell-trainedtothegloryoftheLordandforthepeaceofbothourselvesandthechildrenthemselves?ItistruetheLordpromisesourchildrenshallbetaughtofHimandgreatshallbethepeaceofourchildren.Godhasaskedustoraiseourchildrensothattheywillleadresponsiblelivesafterward(Pro verbs22:6).ToignoreGod'scommandistoexpecttheantithesisofpeace.Maythisnotbeourlot!

RequirementsforResults

Beingeffectiveatparentinginvolvesalotofhardeffort.Itdoesn'tjustcomeeasysincenothingworthwhilecomeseasy.Itbecomesnonethelesslesstaskingthroughthepoweroflove.Loveisgiving,sharing,sacrificing,andpersevering.Itisnotmerelythroughspendingmoneyonchildrenalonelike Joanneerroneouslythough.Ofsure,childtrainingdemandscertainfinancialobligations;butbeyondmoney,good parentingalsorequiresmaterials,mentalawareness,mentoring,molding,mending,andmeticulousness.

Youneedtotravelalongwithyourchildinlovedespitehisskillsandweaknesses.Lovewillmakeyourpardon,pray,protect,provideforandprunehiminagodlyway.Itwillmakeyoucommityourtimetotrainyourchild.Loveisthefuelthatkeepstheengineofparenthoodhumming.Neverallowyouroiloflovetogetdrainedbecauseofobstaclesofchildtraining,householdtasks,matrimonialpainsorgains,oranyotherresponsibilitiesyoucouldbeengagedin.

Lovingyourchildrenwillmakeyoubringthemupwiththerightteachingandpatternofgodlyconduct.Veryvital,toletyouryoungsterrealizetheimportanceofprayer.Teachhimhowtopray.Allowhimtobeprayinginyourpresence,andpermithimtoleadprayerduringthedevotionorprayermeetingathome.Bepatientwithhimthough.Toleratehimevenwhenitlooksunusual,andrememberheislearningfromyou.Teachhimallimportantthingssuchasacademicworkasidefromgoingtoschool,householdchores,godlyculture,morals,excellentbehaviors,andattitude,etc.Noinvestmentyoumakein tokidtrainingislost;youwillun doubtedlygettheadvantages.

RoleofRegeneration

ChildrenarestatedtobeGod'sh eritage(Psalm127.3).(Psalm1 27.3).Heisthefinesttrainerofy oungsters.Weparentsaremere co-

trainerswithHim.Successfulc hildtrainingconsequentlydem andsthatwefollowGod'sbluep rint.Manychildrenarewaywar dbecauseofthefailureoftheirp arentstofollowGod'spatternof childupbringing.Godownsthe child;weparentsareonlycareta kers.Therefore,itneedsabsolu teobediencetoGodtoraiseasuc cessfulchild.

ThefearoftheLordisthebeginn ingofwisdom;wemustseektor aiseourchildreninthewayofth eLord.LeadingachildtoChrist inhisearlylifesafeguardshimfr omtherotinsocietyandprepare shimforexcellenceinlife.Maki ngyouryoungstervalueGod,H isword,prayer,andGod'sminis terswouldaidinmoldingyourc hildforgreatness.Manywayw ardchildrenareoffspringofthe faultyfoundationofgodlessne ssornotgivingGodtherightpos itionintheirfamilieslaidbythe parents.AsthePsalmistproperl yquestioned,"Ifthefoundation swereoverthrown,whatcanthe righteousdo?"(Psalm11:3).

ResiliencedespiteResistance

Thereareoccasions,nodoubtwhentheattitudeofyourchildtoyournurturingattemptsseemsdisrespectfulandprovocative.Butthisshouldnotstopyoufromcontinuingtoadoreyourchild.Letyourlovestaysteady.Expressyourdisgustatanyrevoltingbehaviorouryoungsterexhibitsbutneverdemonstratehatredinanymannerforthechild.

Itcouldalsobethattheyoungsterseemsfrailordelicateornotasintelligentorsmartasyouexpect.Neverloseyourcalmbecauseo fthis.Ormaybeyouarenotrecei vingenoughsupportfromyour spouseintrainingthechild.Don 'tgetdiscouragednorloseyoura ffection.Yourindividualchall engecouldalsobecriticismfro mpeopleontheholywayoftrain ingyouadopt;don'tbefrustrate dorloseyouraffection. Maybeyourwineofprovidingi srunningout;youarenothaving enoughasyouwishfortraining youryoungster.Don'tloseyour affection,retainyourpeaceand praytoGod.Itcouldbepossible thatyouarenothavingsufficien ttimebecauseofyourtightsche dule;neverquit.Upholdyourre solvetoprovideyourchildthefi nestthatGodgivesyouforhim. Asweareadmonishedin1Cori nthians13:4-7,thekindoflovethatGodexpe ctsofustowardsourchildrenan d,indeed,towardseveryone,is onethat"sufferethlong,andisk ind...isnoteasilyprovoked,thi nkethnoevil;Rejoicethnotinin iquity,butrejoicethinthetruth; Bearethallthings,believethallt hings,hopethallthings,endure thallthings." Lovewillnotallowyoutogiveu ponchildtraininguntilyouacco mplishwhatGodwantsyoutod owithyourchild.Don'tforget,h owever,thatcorrectionispartof loveinparenting.Tolovechildr enisnottopamperthemmindle ssly.Lovewillalsomakeyoufix themandsoontooifyouarecons tantlyavailableforthem.

RelyingontheRedeemer

Mostessential,youneedtodepe ndoneverydayandtotallyonG odandletHimteachyouhowtot rainyourchildren.Mosttimes, youneedtohearfromGod.Wep arentsneedtobespirituallysens itivetoknowthestepstotakeata time.Themethodforonesituati onmaynotworkintheother.So, dailydependonGod.Childrena renotthesameeither.Youneed Godtogiveyoupreciseinstruct ionsonhowtotraineachchild,a seachoneisfearfullyandwonderfullymadebyGod.

Bespirituallyawake,parent.HearGodteachyouhowtotrainyourchildren.BedirectedbyHiswordallthetime.EventhebestofparentswillfailifGodisnotgivenHisprideofpositionintheirchild'strainingefforts.RelyonGod.Thisisthekeysecretofsuccessfulparenting.

Onceagain,whateverthegender,character,orattitudeofyourchildren,lovethemtruly.Thiswillmakeanysacrificeoftimeandattentiondifficulties.Itwillbeathrillinstead.Eventhewaywardonescanbewonoverbylove.Patientlyshowerthemwithaffec tionandyouwillobserveitscontagiouseffect.

Butthen,dearreader,areyouintheloveofGodyourself?Youcannotgivewhatyoudon'thave.ToconceiveachildlikeSamuel,theremustbeamotherlikeHannah.TobirthchildrenlikeJudeandJamesthebloodbrothersofJesusChrist,theremustbeamotherlikeMary.TobreedachildlikeJohnWesley,theremustbeamotherlikeSusanWesley.IfyouneedGod'sloveandgraceinyourlife,thengostraightawaytoHiminprayer.AskHimintoyourlife.John3:16convincedusofGod'ssacrificiallove.Donotdelay.Repentofyourfaultsnow.

RestoringtheRebellious

NevermindifitseemsyouhavefailedattheearlystageofparentinglikeJoanne.Areyourchildrendefiantandwilfulalready?CastyourburdenonJesus.RetraceyourstepslikeJoannedid.Godwillgentlyforgiveandrestoreyourtranquilityandthatofyourchildren.Heisanxiouslywaitingforyoutoreorganizeyourpriorities.Stoprushingafterfleetingthingsattheexpenseofyourchildren'searthlyandeternalpeace.Remember,youwillgiveanaccountofyourstewardshipasaparent.Yourbehaviorasaparentcouldinfluenceyoureverlastin gdestiny,irrespectiveofhowre ligiousyouhavebeen. Areyourchildrenwaywardalre adyviayournegligence?Lovec anandwillbringthemback.Foll owJoanne'sexample.Godwill notdisappointyou.Allyounee dissincererepentance.Tracey ourstepsbackandprayerfully mendthewrongs.Godissuretof orgiveandsortthingsoutforyo u.Youalsoneedtoagonizeinpr ayers(Lamentation2:18- 20).(Lamentation2:18- 20).Thisisnecessaryforallpare nts,whetherthechildrenaredoi ngwellorpoorly.There'snothi ngthatprayercannotdo.Monit oryourchildrenwithprayers.

ReapingtheRewards

Parentingisconnectedwithsacrificebutitisveryrewardingifdonefollowing God'sdesignand blueprints. Timespentonchildrenisincrediblyworthwhile.Ifyougiveitwhatittakestoday,youwillundoubtedlyreapwhatyousowafterward.

Childtrainingisalovelyandgratifyingtask.Itbreedspeace,wealth,preservation,productivity,promotion,purity,andposterity.Ithasearthlyandeverlastingrewards.AstheLordassuresinPsalm128:2,"Forthoushalteatthelaborofthinehands:happ

yshalt"be,anditshallbegoodw iththee."
Well-
trainedchildrenareexcellentas setstotheirparents,church,co mmunity,andnation.Intheold ageofparents,theywouldshow erloveonthembytakingproper careoftheirparents.Childrenw hoareproperlyraisedwillbuild uptheirfamilies,communities, churches,andnation.Societyw illbecalmifchildrenareproperl ytrained,crimewilldecline,an dtherewouldbeeconomicands ocio-
politicaltransformationandpr ogresswhenchildrenareprope rlytrained.

Evenmoreheartteningisthatthefruitsofexcellentparentingarenotsimplyconfinedtoearthlyprosperity.ChildrenwhoknowandserveGodwillbeinheavenatlast.Whatagreatjoyshallitbetoseeallyourchildreninparadise!

So,spendandbespentnurturingeveryoneofyourchildrenuntilthepurposeofGodisfulfilledintheirlife.

Giveitallittakes-youwillbegladyoudid!

www.ingramcontent.com/pod-product-compliance
Lightning Source LLC
LaVergne TN
LVHW012118170826
845678LV00014BA/2992

* 9 7 9 8 3 7 0 1 0 6 2 2 4 *